THE TEN-SECOND REWIND

How to Spot the Manipulation Machine Before You Hit Share

By L. Reynolds Jr.
U.S. Army Veteran

Stop Being Played. Start Thinking Clearly.

THE TEN-SECOND REWIND
How to Spot the Manipulation Machine Before You Hit Share

ISBN: [TO BE ASSIGNED]

First Edition

Published by Reynolds Publishing LLC
San Antonio, Texas

Printed in the United States of America

For information about special discounts for bulk purchases, please contact Reynolds Publishing at [contact information].

Cover design by [Designer Name]
Interior design and layout by [Designer/Service Name]

www.TenSecondRewind.com

For Ben,

and everyone learning to see the strings.

Table of Contents

Introduction: The Siege You Can't See

A long-time friend of mine—I'll call him Ben—reached out to reconnect recently after some years of incidental passing encounters. We are both educated men in our fifties, veterans who served in the U.S. Army together in the early 90s. We've had full careers, raised children, and watched various administrations come and go. Loved serving our country so much, we vowed to do it all over again. Ben is a man I respect, someone with multiple degrees and a passport full of stamps.

Yet, during a casual phone call, Ben asked a question that felt less like a bridge and more like a barrier: "I don't understand why you support those people on the other side?"

Although I was stunned by the question, I clarified my position, which sparked weeks of banter, memes, and messages. The camaraderie between servicemembers goes a long way, which we pride ourselves on. But as we talked, I realized something chilling: even for someone as smart as Ben, the programming went deep. He wasn't just expressing an opinion; he was repeating a script. He told me I was "drinking the Kool-Aid," at one point unaware that he was sipping from a glass of his own.

That's when it hit me: your mind is under a quiet, constant siege, and almost nobody notices the shells landing. Every day, armies of highly paid psychologists, data scientists, and narrative engineers fire precision-guided munitions at your attention, your emotions, and your sense of what's normal. Most people never contemplate being in any form of a battle. These weapons don't look like threats; they look like news, entertainment, or a viral clip your old classmate posted.

This book is your "ten-second rewind"—the deliberate breath between the heartstring and the retweet button. This is your way to analyze the terrain you're operating on. Whether you're 18 or 55, liberal or conservative, progressive or traditional, this guide will help you recognize when your emotions are being weaponized, and your conclusions are being gift-wrapped.

The manipulation affects everyone equally. Both sides of every political divide use the same psychological techniques. The battle is usually much bigger than the singular target of your mind. You already suspect you're being manipulated—and you're right. This book will show you exactly how it works and, more importantly, what you can do about it.

Chapter 1: The Seed and the Soil

From 17th-Century Rome to the 21st-Century Screen

Ben's Question

When Ben asked me why I held my political views, I could have dismissed it as simple disagreement. It's not uncommon that I may pose an opposing view for the sake of discussion. But the more we talked, the more I realized: Ben wasn't questioning my reasoning. He was genuinely confused about how an intelligent person could arrive at conclusions different from his own. The media ecosystem he trusted had presented only one "reasonable" perspective—and mine wasn't it.

I've seen this pattern on both sides of the political divide as well as non-political themes. My conservative friends dismiss any criticism of their preferred leaders as "fake news." My progressive friends view opposing viewpoints as evidence of moral failure. Everyone is convinced they're thinking critically while the other side is brainwashed.

The truth? We're all vulnerable to the same manipulation techniques. This chapter examines where propaganda began and how it evolved into the precision-guided psychological weapon aimed at all of us today.

The Evolution of Influence from 1622 to the Digital Age

The word "propaganda" carries a heavy, almost toxic weight today. Not what one would expect from its simple origins. For many, it conjures images of grainy black-and-white reels or Cold War-era posters warning of enemies within. However, to understand how your newsfeed is being manipulated in present-day, we have to look past the posters and into the soil.

The term itself is not inherently "evil." It comes from the Latin propagare, meaning to spread or sow seeds in a garden. In 1622, Pope Gregory XV established the Sacra Congregatio de Propaganda Fide—the Congregation for the Propagation of the Faith. At its inception, it was a neutral, administrative term for sharing beliefs and sowing the "seeds" of a worldview. It wasn't about deception; it was about distribution—amplifying information to attract a specific outcome.

Historical Examples: The Great Shift from Sowing to Snaring

Over the last century, the "seeds" have changed. We have moved from an era of Information (sharing facts) to an era of Influence (shaping behavior). Three pivotal moments show this evolution:

Example 1: World War I Propaganda (1914-1918)

During WWI, governments on all sides used posters, newspapers, and early film to shape public opinion. The British circulated stories of German soldiers committing atrocities—some true, many exaggerated or fabricated—to justify the war effort. The U.S. Committee on Public Information, led by George Creel, created the "Four Minute Men" who gave short, emotionally charged speeches in theaters nationwide. The goal wasn't complex reasoning; it was immediate emotional response: fear, patriotism, rage.

The Tactic: Use anecdotal horror stories to bypass rational analysis.

The Modern Parallel: Viral videos showing isolated incidents framed as representative of entire movements or demographics.

Example 2: Nazi Germany's Propaganda Ministry (1933-1945)

Joseph Goebbels' Ministry of Propaganda didn't just tell Germans what to think—it controlled every channel of information. Radio broadcasts, films like "Triumph of the Will," and carefully staged rallies created an "illusion of consensus." Dissenters were silenced, and repetition made the party's messages feel like universal truth. The technique was simple: saturate every media space with the same message until questioning it feels like insanity.

The Tactic: Control all information channels and repeat the same phrases until they become "common sense."

The Modern Parallel: Coordinated messaging across news outlets, social media influencers, and political pundits using identical talking points within hours of each other. More recently, political leaders have directly stated the media and social media has been effectively used to carry out information saturation.

Example 3: Cold War Psychological Operations (1947-1991)

Both the United States and Soviet Union perfected "psychological operations" (psyops) designed to influence foreign populations. The CIA's Operation Mockingbird allegedly involved relationships with journalists to shape American media narratives. The KGB's "active measures" spread disinformation designed to destabilize Western societies. Both sides understood that the most effective propaganda doesn't look like propaganda—it looks like independent journalism, organic cultural movements, or grassroots activism.

The Tactic: Make propaganda look organic and independent rather than state-directed.

The Modern Parallel: Astroturf campaigns—manufactured "grassroots" movements funded by corporations or governments but presented as spontaneous citizen activism. Social media bot networks amplifying specific narratives to create false impressions of popularity. Bot networks have an early and long history of effective, sophisticated initiatives.

How This Affects You Today

In the past, propaganda was a blunt instrument—a loud megaphone used by a central state. Today, it is a surgical scalpel, A/B tested by algorithms to find the exact crack in your individual psychology. The target of the battle is the same though the techniques have advanced.

For younger adults (18-35), manipulation often looks like "The Aesthetic." It's not a government broadcast; it's a carefully curated lifestyle post or a "hot take" on TikTok that feels organic but is actually part of a focus-grouped narrative. For established professionals and parents (36-55), it often manifests as "The Outrage"—headlines that confirm your deepest fears about "the other side," designed to make you hit "Share" before your rational brain can finish reading the second paragraph. Everyone is subjected to the targeting, no one is immune; and no weapon appears to be off limits.

Note: Throughout this book, when we refer to "younger adults" or "established professionals," we're describing age groups and generational media habits—not political affiliations. The manipulation techniques target psychological patterns, not party membership.

The Invisible Bouncer and Your Digital Garden

Why does this work so effectively on all of us, regardless of age or political affiliation? Because the narrative engineers have mapped the "soil" of the human brain. Every person has what I call an Invisible Bouncer—the psychological mechanism of Confirmation Bias. Confirmation bias acts as a selective gatekeeper for your personal agency—your ability to intentionally act and influence your own life.

Think of your mind as an exclusive club. Information that agrees with your current identity—your political tribe, your values, your fears—is waved through the velvet ropes without an ID check. But information that challenges you? The Bouncer puts up a hand and tells it to get lost. You are exercising your agency to use the information, so it aligns with your identity. Modern propaganda doesn't try to fight the Bouncer; it simply dresses up its messages in the "outfit" the Bouncer is already looking for.

Your First Line of Defense

The goal of this book is to help you recognize the "strings." When you understand that your anger is often a "product" being sold back to you, you gain the power to stop being a "responder" and start being a thinker. It starts with looking at the soil of your own mind and asking: Who planted this thought?

What Ben and I Both Needed to Learn

Ben and I still don't agree on everything. But our ongoing conversations have taught us both to recognize the manipulation tactics that target people across the political spectrum. When he sends me "proof" from his preferred news sources, I can now spot the tells: the recycled talking point, the selectively edited clip, the outrage bait dressed up as journalism. And I've learned to see the same patterns in my own media diet.

The siege isn't going away. This battle is akin to the classic 'Supply and Demand' economic model where the quantity of goods could be replaced with the quality of the technique. The narrative engineers will continue to refine their methods. But you don't have to stand there defenseless while the arrows fly over your head.

Chapter 2: The Invisible Bouncer

The Science of Confirmation Bias and the Digital Gatekeeper

When Ben Challenged My Sources

During one of our debates, Ben sent me an article that "proved" his point about a controversial policy. I immediately noticed it came from a source he'd previously dismissed as biased when I'd cited it. I fervently advocate for understanding the motive of the source. When I pointed this out, he said, "Well, even a broken clock is right twice a day."

I realized I'd done the exact same thing the week before—accepting information from a usually-unreliable source because it confirmed what I wanted to believe. This is the Invisible Bouncer in action: the same source is "credible" when it agrees with us and "biased" when it doesn't.

The Anatomy of the Bias Filter

Imagine you are standing at the entrance of an exclusive club. The music is thumping, the lights are flashing, and there is a long line of people desperate to get inside. At the door stands a massive, unyielding bouncer with a clipboard. He doesn't care how loud someone shouts or how much they wave their arms; if their name isn't on the list, they aren't getting past the velvet rope.

Inside your head, a version of this scene plays out every single time you open your phone, turn on the news, or listen to a friend's "hot take" on a trending topic. You aren't a blank slate. You are a collection of decades of socialization—the silent observations of your parents, the culture of your hometown, and the repeated themes of the media you've consumed including your favorite cartoon. These experiences have created your "Internal Bouncer": your Bias Filter.

At its core, the Invisible Bouncer's job is to protect your identity. Your brain seeks to minimize "cognitive dissonance"—that uncomfortable feeling when new information contradicts your core beliefs. For greatest affect, the mental alarm that ring when something sneaks past your filter and contradicts your worldview is cognitive dissonance. To avoid this stress, the Bouncer uses a "guest list" of your pre-existing values, political leanings, and personal history.

Historical Examples: Confirmation Bias in Action

Example 1: The Salem Witch Trials (1692-1693)

In colonial Massachusetts, once the community accepted the premise that witches existed among them, every piece of evidence was interpreted through that lens. Strange behavior? Witchcraft. Crop failure? Witchcraft. A pig died? Witchcraft. Exculpatory evidence was dismissed or reinterpreted to fit the prevailing narrative. The confirmation bias was so strong that even "spectral evidence"—testimony about dreams and visions—was admitted in court.

The Tactic: Once a community accepts a premise, all evidence is filtered through that belief.

The Modern Parallel: Conspiracy theory communities where every news event is interpreted as "proof" of the conspiracy, and contrary evidence is dismissed as disinformation.

Example 2: The Dreyfus Affair (1894-1906)

In France, Captain Alfred Dreyfus, a Jewish military officer, was convicted of treason based on weak evidence. Even when proof emerged that another officer was the actual spy, military officials refused to admit error. Anti-Semitic prejudice created such strong confirmation bias that authorities literally fabricated additional "evidence" rather than acknowledge they'd imprisoned an innocent man.

The Tactic: Institutions double down on false beliefs rather than admit error, manufacturing evidence to support existing conclusions.

The Modern Parallel: Media outlets or political figures who, when presented with contradictory evidence, attack the source rather than address the substance—and their supporters accept these attacks without examining the underlying facts. This is easy to identify as the tendency is towards a personal attack.

Example 3: The Satanic Panic (1980s-1990s)

During the 1980s, America experienced widespread panic about supposed Satanic ritual abuse in daycare centers. Despite the complete absence of physical evidence, hundreds of people were investigated and dozens imprisoned based primarily on coached testimony from children. Psychologists, social workers, prosecutors, and media outlets all interpreted ambiguous evidence through the lens of the panic. When investigations eventually found no evidence of organized Satanic abuse, many still insisted the conspiracy must be true—they just hadn't found the proof yet.

The Tactic: Once moral panic takes hold, lack of evidence becomes "proof" the conspiracy is being concealed, not that it doesn't exist.

The Modern Parallel: Social media-driven moral panics where ambiguous incidents are immediately interpreted as confirming worst fears, and calls for restraint are dismissed as complicity.

Rage-Baiting: Hacking the Bouncer Across Generations

Narrative engineers understand that the Bouncer is most easily distracted by intense emotion—specifically Rage-Baiting. This content is designed to trigger your emotional center (the amygdala) to bypass your rational filter. However, the "bait" used often appears in very different forms.

For Younger Adults: The Moral Superiority Trap

For digital natives, rage-baiting often centers on "The Aesthetic of Justice." The goal isn't just to make you angry; it's to make you feel morally superior for being angry. A 15-second clip shows a "villain" (representing an opposing group) taken entirely out of context. You infer that this single action represents the entire group's inherent flaws. You share the clip to signal your values to your "tribe," inadvertently acting as a "parrot" for a narrative crafted to keep you engaged.

For Established Professionals: The Fear of Loss

For established professionals and parents, rage-baiting focuses on the "Threat to the Norm." The goal is to make you feel that the world you know is being dismantled. A headline uses an anecdotal hook—a single story of system failure or cultural change presented as an unstoppable wave. The Bouncer lets this in because it confirms your existing anxiety. You engage with the content out of protective duty, unaware that your stress response is being harvested for profit.

The Amygdala Hijack vs. The Ten-Second Rewind

Propaganda is a "precision-guided munition" aimed at your emotions. When you are in a state of high emotion, your Prefrontal Cortex (the part of your brain that does logic and critical thinking) effectively shuts down. You are no longer a rational citizen; you are a responder.

The only way to take back control is the Ten-Second Rewind. By forcing a ten-second pause before you react, comment, or share, you manually "reboot" your Prefrontal Cortex. You give the Bouncer a second to actually check the credentials of the information.

- Ask the Bouncer: "Am I believing this because it's true, or because it makes me feel like I'm winning?"
- Spot the String: "Who benefits from my anger right now?"

What Ben and I Discovered About Our Own Bouncers

Ben and I started comparing notes on our respective "trusted sources." We discovered something humbling: we both had an Invisible Bouncer working overtime. When I questioned his sources, he felt defensive. When he questioned mine, I felt defensive. But once we acknowledged that we both had this bias filter, we could start examining our beliefs more honestly.

The goal isn't to eliminate the Bouncer—that's impossible. The goal is to recognize when he's being manipulated by narrative engineers who understand your psychology better than you do.

Chapter 3: Ghosts in the Machine

The Legal "Firewall" and the Era of Domestic Influence

When Ben Questioned My Conspiracy Theory

During one light-hearted exchange, I mentioned the Smith-Mundt Act and how its modification changed the information landscape. Ben immediately pushed back: "That sounds like a conspiracy theory. You think the government is running propaganda on its own citizens?" Ben then acknowledged he was unfamiliar with the specific law.

I realized how this sounded—like paranoid rambling. But the changes to information regulations aren't theory; they're documented legislative history. Both liberal and conservative media outlets, foreign and domestic institutions, and private corporations now operate in an environment where the old legal guardrails have been removed. This isn't about "the government"—it's about understanding how information flows in an age where the walls between foreign influence operations and domestic media have largely dissolved.

The Smith-Mundt Act of 1948

To understand why your newsfeed feels like a battlefield, we have to look at the legal "firewalls" that used to exist. For over sixty years, the U.S. government operated under a strict legal boundary: it could influence audiences abroad, but it was strictly forbidden from directing those same "information operations" at its own citizens.

At the dawn of the Cold War, the U.S. realized it was losing the "war of ideas." In response, Congress passed the United States Information and Educational Exchange Act of 1948, better known as the Smith-Mundt Act, which was the second congressional attempt to address the issues. The goal was simple: tell the American story to the world to counter Soviet narratives.

However, lawmakers were deeply suspicious of the power of state-run media. They feared that a government capable of influencing the world could easily turn those same psychological tools on its own voters. To prevent this, they built a "firewall": agencies like Voice of America could broadcast to global audiences, but this material was legally banned from distribution within the United States.

Historical Examples: When Governments Controlled Information

Example 1: Operation Mockingbird (1950s-1970s, alleged)

According to various journalistic investigations and limited declassified documents, the CIA allegedly cultivated relationships with American journalists during the Cold War to influence domestic news coverage. While the full extent remains debated, the Senate Church Committee investigations in the 1970s revealed that intelligence agencies did have undisclosed relationships with media figures. Whether formally organized or informal, these relationships blurred the line between independent journalism and government messaging.

The Tactic: Covertly influence media through personal relationships rather than official channels.

The Modern Parallel: Government officials, corporate PR teams, and political campaigns cultivating relationships with journalists and social media influencers who amplify their messaging—sometimes with financial compensation, sometimes through access and exclusivity.

Example 2: Chinese Information Control (2010s-Present)

China's approach to information control demonstrates what happens when governments have unrestricted power to shape domestic narratives. The "Great Firewall" blocks foreign websites, surveillance technology monitors citizen communication, and AI algorithms automatically censor content deemed politically sensitive. State media coordinates messaging across platforms, and social credit systems punish citizens who share "incorrect" information. The result is a population where self-censorship becomes automatic.

The Tactic: Combine technological control with social penalties to create a population that polices itself.

The Modern Parallel: Platform algorithms that suppress certain content, "fact-checking" systems that label information without transparent criteria, and social media mob campaigns that punish users for expressing unpopular views—creating self-censorship through fear of social consequences rather than legal penalties. The initiatives have their greatest affect on developing minds but work very well on the whole population.

Example 3: Russia's "Firehose of Falsehood" (2010s-Present)

Russian information operations, particularly through outlets like RT (formerly Russia Today) and social media operations, use a strategy researchers call the "firehose of falsehood." Rather than carefully constructing a single, coherent narrative, they flood the information space with contradictory stories, half-truths, and outright fabrications. The goal isn't to make people believe a specific lie—it's to make them doubt the possibility of truth itself. Once people can't distinguish fact from fiction, they default to believing whatever confirms their existing biases.

The Tactic: Flood the zone with so much contradictory information that exhausted audiences give up on finding truth.

The Modern Parallel: The overwhelming volume of conflicting claims on social media, where every story has a counter-story, every expert has a counter-expert, and the sheer exhaustion leads people to retreat into information bubbles where at least the narrative is consistent. Do you notice the consistency which when using social media, your personal interests appear prioritized in news feeds?

The 2012 "Modernization": Removing the Guards

For decades, the Smith-Mundt firewall held. But as the world moved from shortwave radio to the borderless internet, the government argued the old law was "obsolete." In 2012, as part of the National Defense Authorization Act (NDAA) for 2013, the Smith-Mundt Act was "modernized." The legal ban on domestic distribution was effectively lifted.

The result? Information campaigns originally designed for foreign audiences can now be legally consumed by Americans at home. The distinction between "public diplomacy" (telling our story to the world) and "domestic messaging" (telling a story to ourselves) has become fine as frog-hair.

This doesn't mean there's a government conspiracy targeting you specifically. It means the legal and technological infrastructure that once separated foreign influence operations from domestic media has been torn down. Now, narrative engineers—from government agencies, foreign powers, corporations, and political campaigns—all operate in the same borderless information space.

How This Affects Your Feed

Without the Smith-Mundt firewall, you are living in a "post-guardrail" era. This affects people differently depending on their media habits:

For Digital Natives: The Blind Spot. If you grew up with the internet, you're used to everything being "content." You might assume that if a message is on a high-production YouTube channel or viral TikTok, it's just "someone's opinion." You're less likely to recognize when a narrative has been "seeded" by an organization with a specific goal. You must treat your "For You Page" as a potential area of operation for influence campaigns rather than just entertainment.

For Established Professionals: The Trust Gap. If you grew up trusting "The Evening News," the removal of these firewalls can be disorienting. You may still believe there are legal checks preventing institutions from manipulating the domestic narrative. You might assume "it's illegal to lie to us like that," not realizing the legal firewall has been dismantled. You are your own last line of defense now.

Taking Back the Clipboard

The dismantling of the Smith-Mundt firewall means you must apply the Ten-Second Rewind more diligently. When you see a narrative that feels too "perfect"—one that simplifies a complex issue into a single, emotional anecdote—stop and ask:

- Who is the source?
- Is this phrase being "parroted" everywhere?
- Is this narrative trying to bypass my logic to hit my heart?

What Ben and I Learned About Information Firewalls

When I explained the Smith-Mundt changes to Ben, he was initially skeptical—it sounded too much like a conspiracy theory, I confess. But when we both researched the legislative history and saw how information regulations had evolved, we realized something important: this isn't about "the government lying to us." It's about understanding that the old legal protections that once existed have been removed. No one has put forward a thorough examination of what the changes mean to the masses.

Now, whether a narrative comes from a government agency, a foreign power, a corporation, or a political campaign, it all flows through the same digital channels. The firewall is down. We are our own last line of defense. Many without fully understanding the battle is in progress.

Chapter 4: Precision-Guided Emotions

The Amygdala Hijack and the Sensory Siege

When Ben Sent Me That Video

Ben once sent me a short video clip that made him furious. It showed a public official making what appeared to be an outrageous statement. The background music was ominous, the editing was tight, and the caption told you exactly how to feel. I felt my own anger rising as I watched it with suspicion that the clip missed some context.

Then I found the full, unedited speech. The official was actually quoting someone else as an example of a position they disagreed with. The 15-second clip had removed all context, added menacing music, and transformed a reasonable discussion into apparent proof of extremism. When I showed Ben the full video, he was stunned. "They made me feel something that wasn't even real," he said.

That's when we both understood: modern propaganda doesn't primarily target your logic. It targets your nervous system.

The Amygdala Hijack: Your Brain Under Siege

If someone wanted to break into a high-security vault, they wouldn't try to guess the 12-digit code. They would create an emergency—a fire, a medical crisis, a panic—that forces the person with the key to run out of the building, leaving the door wide open.

In information warfare, your prefrontal cortex—the logical, analytical part of your brain—is that vault. It's hard to fool with bad math or weak logic. So narrative engineers skip the "code" and go straight for your "emergency" center: the amygdala.

At the base of your brain sits the amygdala, a small, almond-shaped cluster responsible for your "fight or flight" response. When you feel a surge of fear, outrage, or moral superiority, that's your amygdala taking the wheel. In this state, your prefrontal cortex is effectively offline. Your emotions dictate your capacity to act with direction, intensity, and speed. You're no longer a thinking citizen; you're a responder.

Historical Examples: Emotional Manipulation Across Time

Example 1: The Sinking of the Lusitania (1915)

When a German U-boat sank the British passenger ship Lusitania, killing 1,198 people including 128 Americans, the British government used the tragedy to shift American public opinion toward entering World War I. Propaganda posters showed drowning women and children with emotionally charged slogans. What the posters didn't mention: the Lusitania was carrying munitions, making it a legitimate military target under the rules of war. The emotional manipulation worked—American public sentiment shifted dramatically.

The Tactic: Use tragic imagery and selective context to trigger protective and vengeful emotions.

The Modern Parallel: News coverage that focuses intensely on individual victims to build support for specific policies, while omitting broader statistical context or trade-offs.

Example 2: The "Daisy" Political Ad (1964)

The Lyndon Johnson campaign created one of the most famous political ads in history: a little girl counting daisy petals, followed by a nuclear explosion countdown and mushroom cloud. The ad aired only once but was endlessly discussed. It never mentioned opponent Barry Goldwater by name, but it planted the emotional association: vote for Goldwater and your children will die in nuclear war. The amygdala hijack was so effective that Goldwater's campaign never recovered.

The Tactic: Connect innocent imagery (children, families) with existential threats without making explicit claims.

The Modern Parallel: Political ads and social media posts that juxtapose images of happy families with ominous warnings about "what they want to take from you," triggering fear without specific factual claims. The contrast, as a tool, is intended to force the viewer to see the images in new light. The 'before and after' effect.

Example 3: The "Kony 2012" Viral Campaign

In 2012, a nonprofit released a 30-minute video about Ugandan warlord Joseph Kony that became the fastest-spreading viral video in history. Emotionally manipulative music, footage of suffering children, and a simplified narrative triggered massive emotional response. Millions demanded immediate military intervention. However, critics noted the video oversimplified a complex situation, and Kony hadn't been active in Uganda for years. The emotional manipulation was so effective that these facts barely mattered to the outraged audience.

The Tactic: Use high production value, emotional music, and suffering children to bypass critical thinking about complex geopolitical situations.

The Modern Parallel: Slickly produced viral videos about international conflicts or domestic issues that use emotional manipulation to create urgency for specific policy responses, with complex context buried or absent.

The Sensory Siege: Music, Imagery, and Framing

To trigger an amygdala hijack, narrative engineers use a "sensory siege" to ensure your rational brain never gets a chance to engage:

1. Weaponized Soundscapes: Notice the background music in viral clips or news segments. High-energy, fast-paced beats signal urgency. Low, ominous tones trigger fear. Sweeping patriotic orchestrals trigger protective instincts. Music sets the emotional tone before a single word is spoken.

2. Selective Framing: A camera can be moved a few inches to change a tragedy into a cautionary tale. Propaganda isn't just about what is shown—it's about what is left outside the frame. This type manipulation is extensive to include color management, reforming, and image doctoring to depict events that never happened. If the full context would engage your logic, it's removed.

Breaking the Hijack: The Ten-Second Rewind

The only way to defeat a precision-guided emotional attack is to manually reboot your rational brain. When you feel that "heat" in your chest—the urge to scream at a screen or immediately share a post—count to ten.

Ask: "Who benefits from my anger right now?" This forces a shift in perspective. Instead of being consumed by emotion, you engage your prefrontal cortex. Often you'll discover that the primary beneficiaries are not you or the pursuit of truth, but rather the person or entity that provoked the response.

What Ben and I Both Needed to Understand

After the incident with the edited video, Ben and I came to an agreement—an oath: whenever we send each other "proof" of something, we now include the full context and source. The goal is first and foremost to seek the truth. We both realized we'd been sharing emotionally manipulative content without realizing it. The amygdala hijack doesn't just affect "the other side"—it affects everyone who has a nervous system.

By mastering the pause, you move from being a responder to being a thinker. You execute your personal agency with clear thinking. And a thinker is something a narrative engineer can never truly control.

Chapter 5: Weaponized Inference

Leading the Mind Home Without a Map

When Ben "Connected the Dots"

Ben once sent me a series of articles about a political controversy. "Look at the pattern," he said. "It's obvious what's really going on." He hadn't sent me explicit analysis—just a collection of facts that, when arranged a certain way, seemed to point to an undeniable conclusion. (For example, not related to Ben's article, a one-hundred percent increase in marbles lost doesn't necessarily indicate a new travesty when your bag is missing 2 of 1000 marbles—its an increase of one marble)

What struck me wasn't whether his conclusion was right or wrong. It was how certain he was that he'd figured it out himself. The articles hadn't told him what to think—they'd just laid out breadcrumbs in a very specific pattern. He'd drawn the conclusion "independently," which made him far more confident in it than if someone had simply stated it outright.

I realized I'd fallen for the same technique countless times. This is Weaponized Inference: the art of making someone believe an idea was their own.

The "Gift-Wrapped" Conclusion

The most dangerous ideas aren't the ones shouted through a megaphone. They are the ones whispered into the gaps of a story, waiting for your brain to fill them in.

In the world of high-level persuasion, stating a conclusion directly is considered "amateur hour". If a narrative engineer tells you exactly what to think, your internal bouncer might get suspicious. But if they simply provide a carefully curated trail of breadcrumbs and let you arrive at the conclusion yourself, you won't just believe the idea—you will own it.

Traditional propaganda was loud and instructional; it told you what to think. Weaponized inference is quiet and architectural; it builds the house and waits for you to walk inside.

Historical examples from the Protocols of the Elders of Zion to McCarthyism to modern deepfakes all share this pattern: present carefully selected information and let the target draw the "obvious" conclusion themselves.

What Ben and I Learned About "Connecting Dots"

After our conversation about inference, Ben and I started being more careful about how we presented information to each other. Instead of sending articles and saying "see the pattern?", we now explicitly state what conclusion we're drawing and why. This forces us to examine whether the conclusion truly follows from the evidence.

Chapter 6: The Human Shield

Anecdotes vs. Statistics

When Sarah's Story Changed Everything

Ben sent me a heartbreaking news story about a woman named Sarah who had suffered because of a specific policy. The article was devastating—detailed, personal, and undeniably real. "How can you support this policy," Ben asked, "when it does this to people like Sarah?"

I looked up the statistics. Data showed that while cases like Sarah's existed, they represented less than 2% of outcomes. But when I sent Ben the data, he responded: "So Sarah doesn't matter? You're willing to sacrifice her for your statistics?"

The article had used Sarah as a "human shield"—making any discussion of broader data seem callous. And I'd done the same to Ben with different issues.

The Power of the One Over the Million

Your brain is designed to process stories, not spreadsheets. You cannot feel a statistic, but you can feel empathy for one person whose name you know. This is "The Identifiable Victim Effect"—we will move mountains for one person with a face and name but ignore statistics about millions.

In narrative engineering, the "Human Shield" is the strategic use of a single, heart-wrenching anecdote to protect a broader agenda. By the time you finish hearing the personal story, your logic center has shut down and the entire narrative has been waved through.

What Ben and I Learned About Sarah

Ben and I had a long conversation about Sarah and others like her. We acknowledged that her suffering was real and mattered. But we also agreed that policy decisions need to be based on evidence about what helps the most people, not just what feels right in response to one story.

Chapter 7: The Illusion of Consensus

The Science of Parroting and Manufactured Reality

When Ben and I Both Heard the Same Phrase

During a conversation, Ben and I realized we'd both used the exact same eight-word phrase to describe a current event—neither of us could remember where we'd heard it first. Within 24 hours, we saw that phrase on news broadcasts, social media, and even overheard it at a coffee shop. It felt like "everyone" was saying it, which made it feel true.

We researched the phrase and found it had been seeded simultaneously across dozens of media outlets. The "consensus" was manufactured. We'd both been parrots without realizing it.

The "Illusion of Truth" Effect

Our brains have a dangerous glitch: we mistake repetition for truth. If a statement is repeated enough times, the Invisible Bouncer stops checking credentials and waves it through as "common knowledge." Modern propaganda doesn't try to convince you with one powerful argument—it repeats the same phrase until your brain accepts it automatically.

What Ben and I Learned About Parroting

Ben and I now pause when we notice ourselves using a phrase that feels too polished or catchy. We search for it in quotes. If it appears word-for-word across multiple unrelated sources, we know we're looking at manufactured consensus. When you stop parroting the script, you stop being a responder and start being a thinker.

Chapter 8: Ancient Strategies for a Digital Age

Timeless Manipulation Techniques

When Ben Asked About History

Ben once asked me, "Is this manipulation stuff really new, or have humans always done this?" I realized the answer was both. The technology is new, but the psychological techniques are ancient. Studying historical examples—from religious texts to ancient politics—shows that propaganda isn't a modern invention; it's a fundamental part of human communication that predates mass media by millennia.

The Serpent in the Garden

The first recorded instance of "Weaponized Inference" occurs in the Garden of Eden. The Serpent doesn't start with a blatant lie; he starts with a question designed to bypass trust: "Did God really say...?" By focusing on the one restricted thing, he makes the vast freedom of the Garden disappear. He leads Eve to infer that God is withholding something good. This is identical to how modern rage-baiting works—using a single restriction to make an entire system feel oppressive.

Absalom at the Gate

In 2 Samuel, King David's son Absalom provides a masterclass in using anecdotal hooks to build a false narrative. He would stand at the city gate and listen to individual grievances, telling people "Your claims are good and right, but there is no one from the king to hear you." He used these personal stories to build a narrative of administrative incompetence without having any better policy. He "stole the hearts of the people" by acting as a mirror for their frustrations—exactly like modern politicians or pundits who validate specific fears to build movements based on emotion rather than evidence.

The Trial of Jesus

The trial of Jesus before Pilate shows the Illusion of Consensus in action. The religious leaders didn't just present a legal case; they "stirred up the crowd" to create a chorus of voices parroting "Crucify him!" Pilate, a man of logic and law, was overwhelmed by the sheer volume of repetition. The mob's amygdala hijack bypassed the legal firewalls of the Roman system.

What Ben and I Learned From Ancient Examples

Ben and I realized that understanding these ancient patterns helps us recognize modern variations. The playbook hasn't changed in thousands of years because human psychology hasn't changed. Once you see the ancient strings, you can begin to cut the modern ones.

Chapter 9: The Ten-Second Rewind

Your Action Plan

The Science of the Pause

We have explored the "invisible bouncers," the "precision-guided munitions," and the "human shields" of modern persuasion. You now know that the goal of the narrative engineer isn't necessarily to make you believe a lie; it's to make your heart beat just a little bit faster than your brain can fact-check.

How do you fight back? You don't need a degree in data science. All the armor you really need is found in one deliberate breath between the heartstring and the retweet button.

Your Intellectual Self-Defense Drill

The next time you feel that surge of emotion, run this 10-second diagnostic:

- Check the Hook: Is this using a person to bypass data?
- Check the Frame: What was left out?
- Check the Script: Have I heard these exact words from five sources?
- Check Who Benefits: Does my anger align with someone else's profit?

Building the Infrastructure of Truth

The siege isn't going away. But you no longer have to stand there defenseless. By building the "muscle" of the rewind, you become your own last line of defense. You aren't just a "responder" anymore. You are a thinker. And a thinker is the one thing a narrative engineer can never truly control.

Afterword: The First Layer of Armor

The conversation with my friend Ben that started this journey wasn't an ending; it was a beginning. It was the moment I realized that even the most educated among us are not immune to the "quiet, constant siege" of modern narrative engineering.

Beyond the Echo Chamber

The goal of this guide was never to tell you what to think or which political tribe to join. It was to give you the tools to recognize when you are being manipulated. Whether the source is a government-funded media campaign, a focus-grouped social media meme, corporate PR, or a political movement, the tactics are remarkably consistent: simplify the complex, weaponize the anecdote, manufacture consensus, and target the heart to bypass the head.

As a sidenote, the principal concepts and histories introduced in this guide are your tools. Engaging with the topic as a practical exercise will enhance your knowledge and develop the skills needed to overcome the challenges of today's propaganda; although the guide is not exhaustive. I've only 'scratched the surface,' in an effort to ensure the reading is easily consumable.

Cutting the Strings: A Final Word About Ben

Ben and I still disagree on plenty. But that was never the point. The "win" isn't in making him see the world exactly as I do; the win is that we're both starting to spot the tells of the manipulation machine together. We call each other out when we share emotionally manipulative content. We question sources. We look for context. We practice the ten-second rewind.

Most importantly, we've learned that critical thinking isn't a political position—it's a discipline. Truth qualifies opinion and builds the thinking muscles. Critical thinking requires constant vigilance, intellectual humility, and the willingness to be wrong.

Take a breath. Spot the frame. Cut the strings. The clipboard is back in your hands.

Glossary of Terms

Term	Definition
Amygdala	The almond-shaped cluster responsible for "fight or flight" response.
Anecdote	A single story used to make a message relatable while bypassing statistical evidence.
Astroturfing	Creating fake grassroots movements through paid activists or bot networks.
Confirmation Bias	The tendency to favor information that confirms existing beliefs—the "Invisible Bouncer."
Emotional Hijacking	Using imagery or music to bypass rational thought and trigger the amygdala.
Illusory Truth Effect	Believing statements simply because they've been repeated many times.
Propaganda	Information meant to influence emotions and actions rather than encourage critical thinking.
Selective Framing	Deciding which facts the audience sees and in what order.
Smith-Mundt Act	A 1948 legal guardrail against domestic propaganda, modified in 2012.
Ten-Second Rewind	The deliberate breath between the heartstring and the retweet button.

Weaponized Inference Leading an audience to a conclusion without stating it directly.

Appendix: The Media Literacy Checklist

Use this checklist whenever content triggers a strong emotional response.

Before You React

- Apply the Ten-Second Rewind
- Check Your Emotional State
- Identify the "Human Shield"

Evaluate the Source

- Who Created This Content?
- Follow the Money
- Check for Parroting

Examine the Framing

- What's Outside the Frame?
- Notice Sensory Manipulation
- Look for Weaponized Inference

Test Your Biases

- Would I Accept This From the Other Side?
- Check Your Invisible Bouncer
- Seek Opposing Views

Verify Before Amplifying

- Find the Primary Source
- Check for Deceptive Editing
- Verify With Multiple Sources
- Look for Corrections

The Ultimate Question

Who benefits from my anger, fear, or moral certainty right now?

Take a breath. Spot the frame. Cut the strings.

www.ingramcontent.com/pod-product-compliance
Lightning Source LLC
LaVergne TN
LVHW022032200926
848481LV00007B/2657